My Jewish Year

Cath Senker

PowerKiDS
press
New York

Published in 2008 by The Rosen Publishing Group, Inc.
29 East 21st Street, New York, NY 10010

Copyright © 2008 Wayland/The Rosen Publishing Group, Inc.

First Edition

Picture Acknowledgments:
Art Directors and Trip Photo Library 6 (E. James), 7, 8 (I. Genut), 11 (A. Tovy), 12, 19, 21
(H. Rogers); Circa Photo Library 14, 16, 18, 24 (Barrie Searle); Eye Ubiquitous 15 (Chris
Fairclough), 25 (David Cohen); Heather Angel 20; Nutshell Media Title page (Andy Johnstone),
5 (Yiorgos Nikiteas), 20 (Andy Johnstone); World Religions 4 (Christine Osborne); Panos 27
(Nancy Durrell Mckenna); Sonia Halliday 17, 22, 26 (David Silverman); Z. Radovan, Jerusalem
Cover, 13.

Cover photograph: Children dressed up for the Purim festival in Israel.
Title page: Dressed up for Purim in France.

Library of Congress Cataloging-in-Publication Data

Senker, Cath.
  My Jewish year / Cath Senker. -- 1st ed.
      p. cm. -- (A year of religious festivals)
  Includes bibliographical references and index.
  ISBN-13: 978-1-4042-3732-2 (library binding)
  ISBN-10: 1-4042-3732-1 (library binding)
  1. Fasts and feasts--Judaism--Juvenile literature. I. Title.
  BM690.S434 2007
  296.4'3--dc22
                                              2006028065

Acknowledgments: The author would like to thank Fiona Sharpe, Winston Pickett, Adam Pickett
and Lexi Pickett for all their help in the preparation of this book.

Manufactured in China

Contents

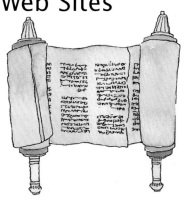

The Jewish people

Jewish people believe there is one God.
He is everywhere and watches over them.

Jews follow the teachings written down
in the Torah, the Jewish holy book.
They also follow many other teachings
of their rabbis.

**A rabbi in synagogue.
Rabbis teach the
Jewish tradition.**

This is Adam. He has written a diary about the Jewish festivals.

Adam's diary
Wednesday, August 13

My name's Adam Pickett. I'm 8 years old. I live with my mom, dad, and sister Lexi— she's 5. We have a cat named Poppet. I like playing soccer. Lexi and I go to the Torah Academy School, which is a Jewish school. I love all the Jewish festivals.

There are rules to help people live a Jewish life. There are also many festivals. Some festivals remind people of events in Jewish history. Others celebrate God's work in creating the world.

The Jewish symbol is the Star of David.

Shabbat in the home

Every Friday

Shabbat is the Jewish day of rest. It is also called the Sabbath. Shabbat lasts from just before sunset on Friday evening until it is dark on Saturday evening.

On Friday evening, families spend time together. Before the sun sets, the mother lights two candles and says a blessing.

Two candles are lit to welcome Shabbat.

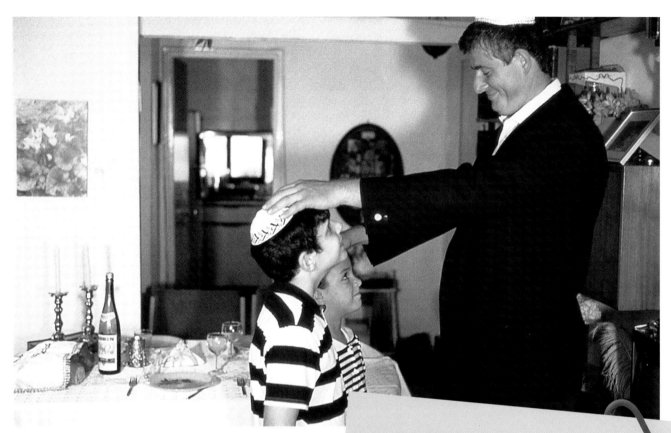

**This father is blessing his children.
The table is set for the Shabbat meal.**

The father blesses
his children. He says
a blessing called
Kiddush over wine.

He blesses the special
bread, called challah.
Then the family eats
a delicious meal.

Adam's diary
Saturday, August 16

Last night, Dad came home
early from work for Shabbat.
This Friday we had visitors,
too. Mom lit the candles and
Lexi helped her. Lexi has her
own small candles to light. Dad
made Kiddush over the wine.
We had chicken for dinner
(sometimes we have lamb
chops). We talked about what
we did during the week.

Shabbat in the synagogue

Every Saturday

Jewish people do not work on Shabbat. They spend a quiet day with their family.

On Saturday morning, they go to synagogue. The rabbi reads from the Torah and gives a sermon. Everyone wishes each other *Shabbat shalom,* meaning "good Sabbath."

These boys are praying in synagogue. The prayer book is written in Hebrew, the Jewish holy language.

This is the Havdalah ceremony. When the candle it lit, Shabbat is over.

Adam's diary
Sunday, August 17

Yesterday, I went to the synagogue with my dad. The rabbi read the Parsha, the weekly part of the Torah. In the evening, we had the Havdalah ceremony to end Shabbat. We lit a candle and put spices on a plate. The spices showed that the sweetness of Shabbat was ending. Everyone sang songs. I held the candle mostly but Lexi had a turn, too.

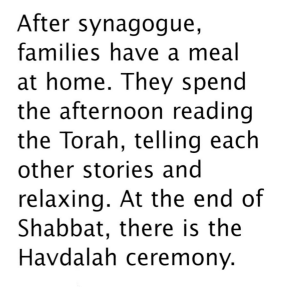

After synagogue, families have a meal at home. They spend the afternoon reading the Torah, telling each other stories and relaxing. At the end of Shabbat, there is the Havdalah ceremony.

Rosh Hashanah

September

Rosh Hashanah is the Jewish New Year. In synagogue the rabbi blows a ram's horn called a shofar. It is like a "wake-up call."

At Rosh Hashanah, Jewish people think about what they have done wrong over the past year.

The rabbi is blowing the shofar in synagogue.

This family is eating a special meal for Rosh Hashanah. There are dates, pumpkin jam, and other sweet fruits.

At home, people eat apples with sweet honey, or food made from carrots or pumpkins. The color orange stands for good luck. Everyone wishes each other a sweet and happy New Year.

Adam's diary
Saturday, September 27

Yesterday, the rabbi at our school blew the shofar in the hall for Rosh Hashanah. Today, we ate apples dipped in honey. I don't like apples and I don't really like honey either, but we always eat them at Rosh Hashanah. I went to synagogue with Mom, Dad, and Lexi. We had loads of visitors and we visited other people too. We ate a lot!

Yom Kippur

September or October

Yom Kippur is the holiest day of the Jewish year. People think about any bad things that they have done over the past year. They say sorry and ask God to forgive them.

On Yom Kippur, mothers of Jewish families light candles just before sunset and the holy day begins. The synagogue is packed. Everyone prays to God.

Adults do not eat or drink for 25 hours. This is called fasting. Children may fast for just part of the day.

The Yom Kippur candle is lit at the beginning of the fast. It stays lit until the end.

Some Jewish men wear a white robe called a kittel for Yom Kippur. It is a sign of being pure.

Adam's diary
Monday, October 6

God has three books: the good book, the bad book, and the middle book. He weighs up the good and the bad things you've done on his scale. If you've had a good year, you go in the good book. If you've had an OK year, you go in the middle book. And if you've had a bad year, you go in the bad book. But God will always forgive you.

Sukkot

September or October

At Sukkot, Jewish people remember their ancestors by building an outdoor shelter. It is called a sukkah.

During Sukkot, families eat their meals in the sukkah. In hot countries they sleep in them, too. They remember how the Jewish people left Egypt long ago.

This boy holds the four plants that are used at Sukkot prayers.

14

These children are decorating the roof of their sukkah with fruit.

The Jews traveled through the desert from Egypt to Israel. When they stopped, they built small huts for shelter. They covered the huts with leaves from palm trees.

Adam's diary

Sunday, October 12

Yesterday was the first day of Sukkot. We made a tiny sukkah at home out of wafers, peanut butter, and pretzels. I went to see my friend Asher's sukkah. It was really cool. His family had decorated it with CDs! We had a sukkah at school, which we decorated with kaleidoscope patterns we had drawn ourselves. The teachers hung up fruit, too, and we shook the Sukkot plants.

Simchat Torah

October

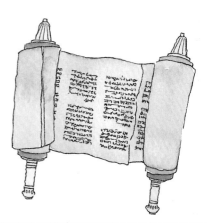

Simchat Torah is a happy day.
The Torah is carried around
the synagogue. Everyone sings
and dances.

The Torah is
very precious.
Every synagogue
has one made
from long scrolls.

The end of each
scroll is stitched
to a wooden pole.
The pole is used to
wind up the scroll.

**At Simchat Torah, people
parade the Torah scrolls
through the synagogue.**

16

People use a pointer called a yad so they don't touch the precious Torah. The Torah is written in Hebrew.

Adam's diary
Saturday, October 18

Today, it was Simchat Torah. We danced around in the synagogue. We sang songs, too. It was really lots of fun. We all got bags of candies at the end. At school, I studied the Torah. I learned some more Hebrew words. I can read some Hebrew already and say a few blessings.

A part of the Torah is read every week in synagogue. At Simchat Torah, the rabbi reads the last part of the Torah and then starts again from the beginning.

Hanukkah

December

At Hanukkah, Jews remember the time long ago when their ancestors stood up to their Greek rulers. Their rulers wanted them to worship many gods. They ruined the Jews' beautiful temple in Jerusalem.

These children are learning to light the Hanukkah candles. Then they will eat some fried doughnuts.

The hanukiah has eight branches and an extra one for the lighting candle.

A brave Jewish group called the Maccabees fought the Greeks and won. They cleaned the temple in Jerusalem and lit their holy lamps. They thought there was only enough oil for one day, but it lasted for eight days—a miracle!

At Hanukkah, Jews light candles on a special candle holder called a hanukiah (menorah).

Adam's diary
Sunday, December 28

Last week at school, we made our own hanukiahs out of clay for Hanukkah. When they were dry we painted them. At home we lit a big hanukiah. We ate latkes (pancakes) fried in oil to remember how in the old days they used oil to light the hanukiah. We got a present every day of Hanukkah, for eight days. It was my birthday at Hanukkah, too.

Tu B'Shvat

January or February

This happy festival celebrates nature. It marks the time in Israel when the rainy season is over. Trees start to grow their new fruit.

Some Jewish people plant trees at Tu B'Shvat. They talk about how they can care for the countryside. Many different kinds of fruit are tasted, too.

This fig tree is growing new fruit.

Jewish people believe that God brings the changes in the seasons. He looks after nature all the time.

Jewish people in many countries plant a tree at Tu B'Shvat. These people are planting a cherry tree in England.

Adam's diary
Sunday, February 8

Yesterday, it was Tu B'Shvat, which is all about trees. People plant new trees. Two years ago, the whole school planted trees and I helped. This year we held a Tu B'Shvat meal with lots of different fruits, like pomegranate. I didn't eat them myself, because I don't like any fruit or vegetables, except for broccoli.

Purim

February or March

Purim is the most cheerful day in the Jewish year. It celebrates the Jewish people who lived in Persia over 2,400 years ago.

At that time, the king of Persia had a chief minister called Haman. He hated the Jews and wanted to kill them. The king agreed. But the king didn't know his wife, Esther, was Jewish.

Jewish people eat cakes called Haman's ears in memory of the Purim story.

These children in France are wearing costumes for Purim.

Esther risked her life by asking the king to save the Jews. Luckily the king changed his mind and the evil Haman was hanged.

Adam's diary
Sunday, March 7

Today, it was Purim. I love Purim because we get to dress up. At school on Friday, I wore a Greek god costume. My mom made it out of a pillow-case. At school, Rabbi Efune read the story of Esther in Hebrew. The story was written in English on the board with pictures. Every time we heard the name "Haman," we banged the chairs.

Pesach

March or April

Pesach is a happy festival. It is also called Passover. It celebrates the Jews' escape from Egypt long ago.

Over 3,000 years ago, the Jewish people were slaves in Egypt. Their leader, Moses, asked the pharaoh to let the Jews go, but he refused.

A family group at Seder night. They are reading the story of Pesach. Then they will eat a special meal.

The Seder plate. It holds special foods that are used to help tell the story of Pesach.

Adam's diary
Wednesday, April 7

Last night was the start of Pesach. We went to Seder night, bringing our own plagues! We took toy frogs and locusts, and red plastic noses to pretend they were boils. When the Jews left Egypt, they didn't have enough time to make proper bread. The dough turned hard and flat, like matzah. That's why we eat matzah every Pesach.

Then the Egyptians were struck by ten terrible plagues. The last one killed their eldest sons.

In the end, the pharaoh told the Jews to leave. There was no time to bake proper bread. So they grabbed flat bread that had not yet risen and quickly left.

Shavuot

May or June

Shavuot is a joyful event. It celebrates the day when God gave the Torah to the Jewish people. This happened seven weeks after they had escaped from Egypt.

At Shavuot, some Jews stay up all night studying the Torah. People decorate the synagogue with flowers. They eat foods made with milk, such as cheesecake and milk pudding.

Here you can see cheesecake (at the front) and cheese-filled pancakes called blintzes (at the back).

Shavuot is also a harvest festival. These people in Israel are celebrating the wheat harvest in the fields.

Young children are given their first Bible storybooks at Shavuot.

Adam's diary
Thursday, May 27

Yesterday was Shavuot. We ate cheesecake and Mom made pancakes filled with cheese. The grown-ups stayed up all night to pray. That's because the night when God gave the Torah to the Jewish people, they arrived late. To make up for it, people study the Torah all night.

Jewish calendar

September (2 days)

Rosh Hashanah

This festival marks the Jewish New Year.

September/October (1 day)

Yom Kippur

People ask God to forgive them for things they have done wrong.

September/October (7 or 8 days)

Sukkot

Families build huts and live in them for a week.

October (1 day)

Simchat Torah

People show their love for the Torah.

December (8 days)

Hanukkah

People light candles to remember how the Jews got their Temple back.

January/February (1 day)

Tu B'Shvat (New Year for Trees)

Jews plant trees and think about how to care for nature.

February/March (1 day)

Purim

People dress up. They hear how Esther helped to save the Jews from the wicked Haman.

March/April (7 or 8 days)

Pesach

People celebrate the Jews' escape from Egypt. They eat matzah instead of bread.

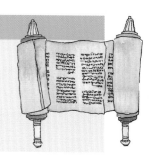

May/June (1 or 2 days)

Shavuot

This festival celebrates God giving the Torah to Moses.

Glossary

blessing A prayer to ask God to protect someone or to thank God for something.

fast To go without food.

hanukiah A candleholder for nine candles. One candle is used to light the others.

Havdalah A ceremony at the end of Shabbat when blessings are said over wine, spices, and a candle.

Kiddush A blessing said over a cup of wine at the beginning of Shabbat and festival meals.

kittel A white robe that men wear over their clothes for Yom Kippur. White is a sign of being pure. The men will be pure when they have said sorry for any bad things they have done.

latkes Potato pancakes.

locusts Large insects that fly in big groups and eat all the plants in an area.

matzah A thin cracker made of flour and water.

pharaoh A ruler of Ancient Egypt.

plague An illness that spreads quickly and kills many people. Also, a large number of animals that come into an area and cause damage.

pomegranate A juicy red fruit that contains many seeds.

rabbi A Jewish religious teacher and leader.

scroll A long roll of paper for writing on.

Seder A meal with a religious ceremony. It usually means the Seder at Pesach.

Shabbat Also called the Sabbath. This is the Jewish day of rest, every Saturday.

sermon A talk, usually about a religious topic, given by a religious leader.

shofar A ram's horn that is blown at the time of Rosh Hashanah.

sukkah An outdoor hut with at least three sides and a roof of leaves.

synagogue A building where Jewish people meet, pray, and study.

Torah The first five books of the Bible. It can also mean all the Jewish teachings.

For Further Reading

Books to Read

Judaism (Religions of the World) by Michael Keene (World Almanac Library, 2006)

Judaism (World Religions) by Ian Graham (Walrus Books, 2005)

Purim (Rookie Read-About Holidays) by Carmen Bredeson (Children's Press, 2003)

The Kids Book of World Religions by Jennifer Glossop (Kids Can Press, 2003)

What You Will See Inside A Synagogue by Lawrence A Hoffman (Skylight Paths Publishing, 2004)

World Religions (History Detectives) by Simon Adams (Southwater, 2004)

Places to Visit

Jewish Museum of Florida

301 Washington Avenue

Miami Beach

Florida, FL 33139

Tel: 305-672-5044

www.jewishmuseum.com

Jewish Museum of New York

1109 Fifth Avenue

New York, NY 10128

Tel: 212.423.3200

www.thejewishmuseum

National Museum of American

Jewish History

Independence Mall East

55 North 5th Street

Philadelphia, PA 19106-2197

Tel: 215-923-3811

www.nmajh.org

Due to the changing nature of Internet links, Powerkids Press has developed an online list of Web sites related to the subject of this book. This site is updated regularly. Please use this link to access the list:
www.powerkidslinks.com/ayrf/jewish/

The author

Cath Senker is an experienced writer and editor of children's information books.

Index

A

ancestors 14, 18

B

blessings 6, 7, 17

C

candles 6, 7, 9,12, 18, 19

challah 7

E

Egypt 14, 15, 24, 25, 26

Esther 22, 23

F

fasting 12

food 7, 9, 11, 18, 19, 22, 24, 25, 26, 27

forgiveness 12, 13

fruits 11, 15, 20, 21

H

Haman 22, 23

hanukiah 19

Hannukah 18, 19

harvest 27

Havdalah 9

Hebrew 8, 17, 23

J

Jerusalem 18, 19

K

Kiddush 7

kittel 13

M

matzah 25

Moses 24

P

palm trees 15

Pesach 24, 25

pharaoh 24

plagues 25

prayers 12, 14

presents 19

Purim 22, 23

R

rabbis 4, 8, 9, 10, 11, 17, 23

Rosh Hashanah 10, 11

S

Seder night 24, 25

Shabbat 6, 7, 8, 9

Shavuot 26, 27

shofar 10, 11

Simchat Torah 16, 17

story 22, 23, 24, 27

sukkah 14, 15

Sukkot 14, 15

synagogue 8, 9, 10, 11, 12, 16, 17, 26

T

temple 18, 19

Torah 4, 8, 9, 16, 17, 26, 27

Tu B'Shvat 20, 21

Y

Yom Kippur 12, 13

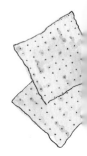